PREFACE

This book is only approved as a helpful resource. It is not intended to be a comprehensive course on the laws of each state. Prior to carrying a firearm into these states, it is solely your responsibility to know all applicable laws.

This book is intended to give you a quick glance at some common questions asked about carrying handguns.

Please make special note of information for the following sections:

Reciprocity: In states that honor permits issued by particular states, there is a map attached.

Legal Permit Age: Some states allow handgun possession by younger ages, but will only accept permits by those of the listed age. Many states also make exceptions for those that are active military. Read the state laws for details that may pertain to you.

Officer Contact – Required To Inform: If you are ever contacted by law enforcement for any reason, It is generally a good idea to inform them if you are carrying concealed, but some states require you to do so.

Open Carry: While this is a right in many states, it generally is not the best practice for many reasons. Some state laws are ambiguous on the subject, which could lead to legal troubles for you, even if you did not intend to violate the law. Before deciding to open carry in a location, thoroughly research the laws for that particular state.

Carry Loaded Handgun In Vehicle: Many state laws are quite vague on this subject, but most recognize the right of a lawful permit holder to have a loaded handgun in their vehicle. Some states outright prohibit this act, unless a person has a permit recognized by that particular state.

Carry Prohibited In These Locations: This is not a comprehensive or exhaustive list. This is simply a list of places that you should know are definitely prohibited if you carry in that state. If you are unsure about whether or not it is legal to carry in a particular location, refer to that state's laws for more details.

- Schools – There is typically an exception made with school parking lots under the following two conditions:
  - Most all states acknowledge that a person with a lawful permit may carry their firearm, as long as they do not exit their personal vehicle.
  - If exiting the vehicle, most states make a provision for a lawful permit holder to lock their firearm in a secure location within their personal vehicle.
- Criminal Justice facility – For the purpose of this book means both law enforcement offices as well as correctional facilities.
- Any place signs prohibit – In states with this listed, this means that it is a crime to carry in such a location. In all other states, private businesses usually have the right to restrict firearms carry, but doing so is not criminal. They simply have the right to ask you to leave while carrying a firearm. Failure to do so would then be the crime of trespassing or similar.
- Liquor establishment – This most commonly refers to a place of business, or <u>section</u> of a business, that serves alcohol, where this makes up at least 51% of the revenue at that location.

Deadly Force Laws: These are a quick reference to some of the laws surrounding use of a firearm in each state. It is your responsibility to know these if you carry there.

Table of Contents

Alabama	5		Montana	30
Alaska	6		Nebraska	31
Arizona	7		Nevada	32
Arkansas	8		New Hampshire	33
California	9		New Jersey	34
Colorado	10		New Mexico	35
Connecticut	11		New York	36
Delaware	12		North Carolina	37
Florida	13		North Dakota	38
Georgia	14		Ohio	39
Hawaii	15		Oklahoma	40
Idaho	16		Oregon	41
Illinois	17		Pennsylvania	42
Indiana	18		Rhode Island	43
Iowa	19		South Carolina	44
Kansas	20		South Dakota	45
Kentucky	21		Tennessee	46
Louisiana	22		Texas	47
Maine	23		Utah	48
Maryland	24		Vermont	49
Massachusetts	25		Virginia	50
Michigan	26		Washington	51
Minnesota	27		West Virginia	52
Mississippi	28		Wisconsin	53
Missouri	29		Wyoming	54

Alabama

Reciprocity: Alabama honors all other state permits

Legal Permit Age: 18 years old

Officer Contact – Required To Inform: NO

Open Carry: Legal

Carry Loaded Handgun In Vehicle: Illegal without permit

Carry Prohibited In These Locations:

- Criminal justice buildings
- Mental health facilities
- Courthouse
- Schools
- Any athletic event not related to firearms
- Any business with "No Gun" sign posted

Deadly Force Laws: Code of Alabama: Section 13

Section 13A-3-20 Definitions.
Section 13A-3-22 Execution of public duty.
Section 13A-3-23 Use of force in defense of a person.
Section 13A-3-24 Use of force by persons with parental, custodial or special responsibilities.
Section 13A-3-25 Use of force in defense of premises.
Section 13A-3-26 Use of force in defense of property other than premises.
Section 13A-3-27 Use of force in making an arrest or preventing an escape.
Section 13A-3-28 Use of force in resisting arrest prohibited.
Section 13A-3-30 Duress.
Section 13A-3-31 Entrapment.

Alaska

Reciprocity: Alaska honors all other state permits

Legal Permit Age: 21 years old

Officer Contact – Required To Inform: YES

Open Carry: Legal

Carry Loaded Handgun In Vehicle: Legal

Carry Prohibited In These Locations:

- Schools
- Liquor establishments
- Public child care facility
- Courthouse
- Any business with "No Gun" sign posted

Deadly Force Laws: Alaska Statute: Section 11.81

AS 11.81.300. Justification: Defense.
AS 11.81.320. Justification: Necessity.
AS 11.81.330. Justification: Non-Deadly Force in Defense of Self.
AS 11.81.335. Justification: Use Deadly Force in Defense of Self.
AS 11.81.340. Justification: Use of Force Defense of a Another
AS 11.81.350. Justification: Use of Force Defense of Property
AS 11.81.400. Justification: Use of Force in Resisting or Interfering with Arrest.
AS 11.81.410. Justification: Use of Force by Guards.
AS 11.81.420. Justification: Performance of Public Duty.
AS 11.81.430. Justification: Use of Force, Special Relationships.
AS 11.81.440. Duress.
AS 11.81.450. Entrapment.

Arizona

Reciprocity: Arizona honors all other state permits

Legal Permit Age: 21 years old

Officer Contact – Required To Inform: NO

Open Carry: Legal (18 years and older)

Carry Loaded Handgun In Vehicle: Legal

Carry Prohibited In These Locations:

- Schools
- Nuclear stations
- Polling places on Election Day.
- Correctional facilities (this includes the parking lot of such facilities).
- Any business with "No Gun" sign posted

Deadly Force Laws: Arizona Revised Statutes: Section 13-400

ARS 13-401 Justification as defense
ARS 13-403 Justification; use of physical force
ARS 13-404 Justification; self-defense
ARS 13-405 Justification; use of deadly physical force
ARS 13-406 Justification; defense of a third person
ARS 13-407 Justification; physical force in defense of premises
ARS 13-408 Justification; physical force in defense of property
ARS 13-411 Justification; use of force in crime prevention
ARS 13-412 Duress
ARS 13-413 No civil liability for justified conduct
ARS 13-414 Justification; use of reasonable and necessary means
ARS 13-415 Justification; domestic violence
ARS 13-417 Necessity defense

Arkansas

Reciprocity: Arkansas honors all other state permits

Legal Permit Age: 21 years old (18 for Military)

Officer Contact – Required To Inform: YES

Open Carry: Legal (still being finalized by court)

Carry Loaded Handgun In Vehicle: Legal if on a "journey"

Carry Prohibited In These Locations:

- Criminal Justice buildings
- Correctional facilities
- Courthouse
- Liquor establishments
- Any athletic event not related to firearms
- Any church or other place of worship
- Any business with "No Gun" sign posted

Deadly Force Laws: Arkansas Code: Section 5-2-600

5-2-601 Definitions.
5-2-602 Defense.
5-2-603 Execution of public duty.
5-2-604 Choice of evils.
5-2-605 Use of physical force generally.
5-2-606 Use of physical force in defense of a person.
5-2-607 Use of deadly physical force in defense of a person.
5-2-608 Use of physical force in defense of premises.
5-2-609 Use of physical force in defense of property.
5-2-614 Use of reckless or negligent force.
5-2-620 Use of force to defend persons and property within home.

California

Reciprocity: California does not honor any other state permits

Legal Permit Age: 21 years old

Officer Contact – Required To Inform: YES

Open Carry: Illegal (still being finalized by court)

Carrying Loaded Handgun In Vehicle: Illegal

Carry Prohibited In These Locations:

- Gun shows
- State capital
- Polling areas
- Liquor establishments
- Any public area while wearing a mask
- Courtrooms

Deadly Force Laws: California Penal Code:

195. Homicide is excusable in the following cases

196. Homicide is justifiable when committed by public officers and those acting by their command in their aid and assistance

197. Homicide is also justifiable when committed by any person in any of the following cases

198. Bare fear

198.5 person using force intended or likely to cause death or great bodily injury within his or her residence

Colorado

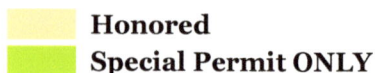

Reciprocity: Colorado honors the following RESIDENT permits

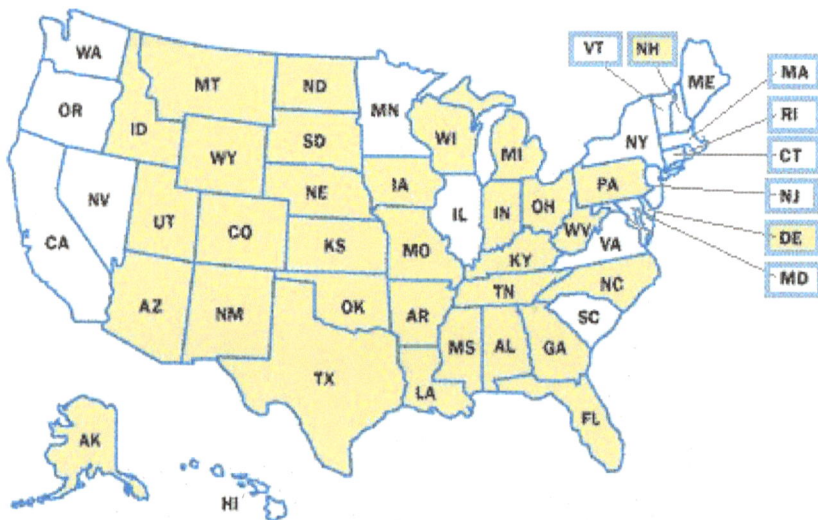

Legal Permit Age: 18 years old

Officer Contact – Required To Inform: NO

Open Carry: Legal (still being finalized by court)

Carrying Loaded Handgun In Vehicle: Legal

Carry Prohibited In These Locations:

- Schools
- Places with security screening devices at entrance

Deadly Force Laws: Colorado Revised Statutes: 18-1-700

Connecticut

Reciprocity: Connecticut does not honor any other state Permits/Licenses

Legal Permit Age: 21 years old

Officer Contact – Required To Inform: NO

Open Carry: Legal w/ Permit

Carrying Loaded Handgun In Vehicle: Illegal

Carry Prohibited In These Locations:

- Schools
- Legislative Buildings

Deadly Force Laws: General Statutes of Connecticut:

Sec. 53a-16. Justification as defense.

Sec. 53a-16a. Affirmative defense: firearms

Sec. 53a-16b. Affirmative defense: co-participant, firearms

Sec. 53a-17. Conduct required or authorized by law

Sec. 53a-18. Use of physical force or deadly physical force

Sec. 53a-19. Use of physical force in defense of person.

Sec. 53a-20. Use of physical force in defense of premises.

Sec. 53a-21. Use of physical force in defense of property.

Sec. 53a-23. Use of physical force to resist arrest not justified.

Delaware

Reciprocity: Delaware honors the following state permits

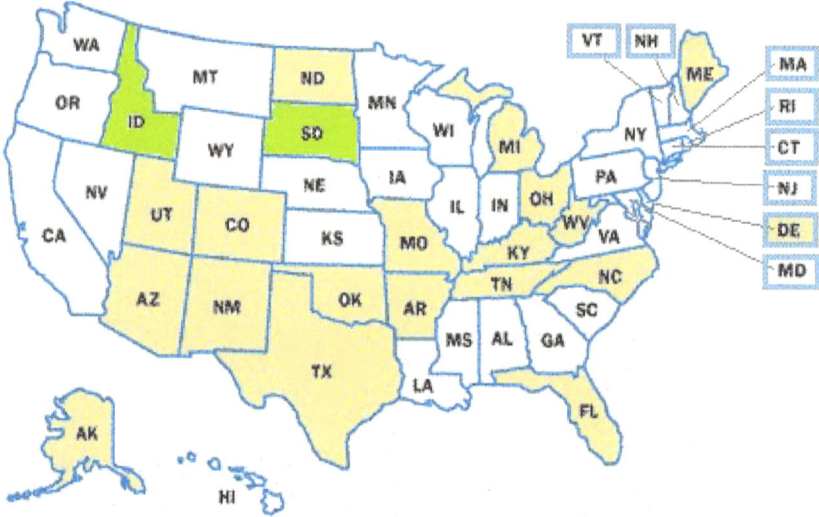

Legal Permit Age: 18 years old

Officer Contact – Required To Inform: NO

Open Carry: Legal

Carrying Loaded Handgun In Vehicle: Illegal

Carry Prohibited In These Locations:

- School buses
- State Parks
- Criminal Justice facilities
- Courts

Deadly Force Laws: Delaware Code: 461-475

Florida

Reciprocity: Florida honors the following RESIDENT Permits

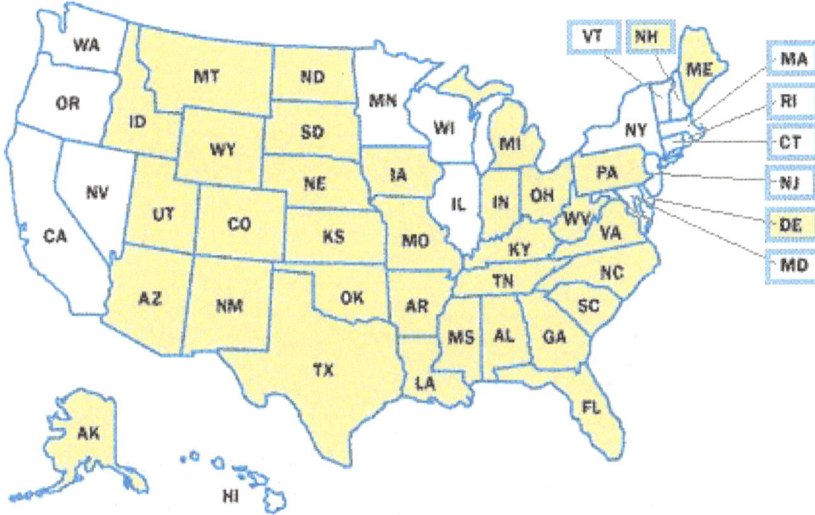

Legal Permit Age: 21 years old

Officer Contact – Required To Inform: NO

Open Carry: Illegal

Carrying Loaded Handgun In Vehicle: Illegal

Carry Prohibited In These Locations:

- Schools
- Criminal Justice facilities
- Polling places
- Mental health facilities

Deadly Force Laws: Florida Statutes: Section 776

Georgia

Reciprocity: Georgia honors the following state Permits

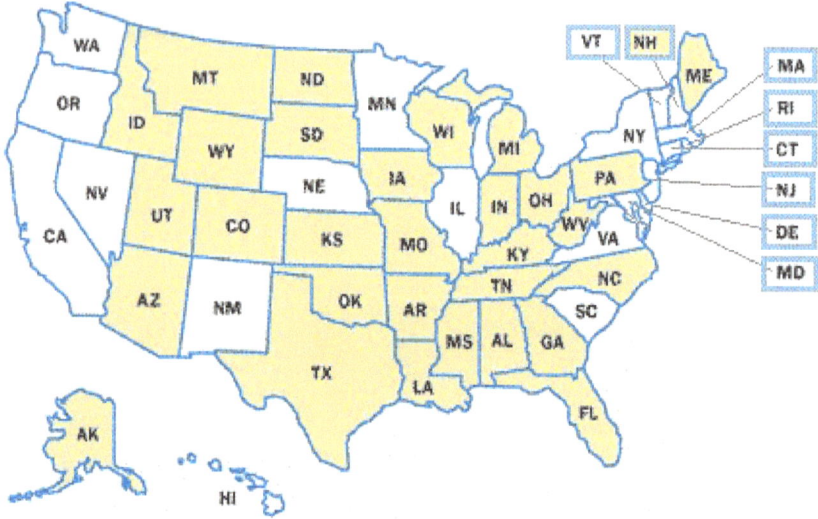

Legal Permit Age: 21 years old

Officer Contact – Required To Inform: NO

Open Carry: Legal w/ Permit

Carrying Loaded Handgun In Vehicle: Legal

Officer Contact – Required To Inform: NO

Carry Prohibited In These Locations:

- Schools / School buses
- Criminal Justice facilities
- Churches or places of worship
- Mental health facilities
- Government buildings

Deadly Force Laws: Code of Georgia: Section 16-3

Hawaii

Reciprocity: Hawaii does not honor any other state permits

Legal Permit Age: 21 years old

Officer Contact – Required To Inform: NO

Open Carry: Illegal

Carrying Loaded Handgun In Vehicle: Illegal

Carry Prohibited In These Locations:

- None specifically listed

Deadly Force Laws: Hawaii Revised Statutes: Section 703-300

§703-300 Definitions relating to justification.

§703-301 Justification a defense; civil remedies unaffected.

§703-302 Choice of evils.

§703-303 Execution of public duty.

§703-304 Use of force in self-protection.

§703-305 Use of force for the protection of other persons.

§703-306 Use of force for the protection of property.

§703-307 Use of force in law enforcement.

§703-308 Use of force to prevent suicide or the commission of a crime.

§703-309 Use of force by persons with special responsibility for care, discipline, or safety of others.

§703-310 Provisions generally applicable to justification

Idaho

Reciprocity: Idaho honors all other state permits

Legal Permit Age: 21 years old

Officer Contact – Required To Inform: NO

Open Carry: Legal

Carrying Loaded Handgun In Vehicle: Legal

Carry Prohibited In These Locations:

- Schools
- Courts
- Juvenile justice facility

Deadly Force Laws: Idaho Statutes: Section 19-200

19-201 Lawful Resistance

19-202 Resistance by Threatened Party

19-202a Legal Jeopardy in Cases of Self-Defense and Defense of Other Threatened Parties

19-203 Resistance by Other Parties

19-204 Prevention of Offenses by Officers of Justice

19-205 Prevention by Persons Assisting Officers

Illinois

Reciprocity: Illinois does not honor any other state permits

Legal Permit Age: 21 years old

Officer Contact – Required To Inform: NO

Open Carry: Illegal

Carrying Loaded Handgun In Vehicle: Illegal

Officer Contact – Required To Inform: NO

Carry Prohibited In These Locations:

- Schools
- Hospitals
- Mental health facilities
- Public park or playground
- Government building
- Criminal Justice facility
- Courts
- Liquor establishments
- Library
- Museum
- Zoo
- Stadium or arena
- Nuclear energy facilities
- Riverboat gaming facility

Deadly Force Laws: Illinois Compiled Statutes: Section 7

Indiana

Reciprocity: Indiana honors all other state permits.

Legal Permit Age: 18 years old

Officer Contact – Required To Inform: NO

Open Carry: Legal w/ Permit

Carrying Loaded Handgun In Vehicle: Illegal

Carry Prohibited In These Locations:

- Schools
- Riverboat gaming facility
- Race track
- State fair

Deadly Force Laws: Indiana Code: Section 35-41-3

35-41-3-2 Use of force to protect person or property

35-41-3-3 Use of force relating to arrest or escape

35-41-3-5 Intoxication

35-41-3-6 Mental disease or defect

35-41-3-7 Mistake of fact

35-41-3-8 Duress

35-41-3-9 Entrapment

Iowa

Reciprocity: Iowa honors all other state permits

Legal Permit Age: 21 years old*

*18 if needed in course of employment

Officer Contact – Required To Inform: NO

Open Carry: Legal w/ Permit

Carrying Loaded Handgun In Vehicle: Illegal

Officer Contact – Required To Inform: NO

Carry Prohibited In These Locations:

- Schools
- School buses
- State buildings
- Casino
- State fair

Deadly Force Laws: Iowa Code: Section 704

Kansas

Reciprocity: Kansas honors all other state permits

Legal Permit Age: 21 years old

Officer Contact – Required To Inform: NO

Open Carry: Legal

Carrying Loaded Handgun In Vehicle: Legal

Carry Prohibited In These Locations:

- Schools
- Criminal Justice facilities (secure areas)
- Any place where signs are posted

Deadly Force Laws: Kansas Statutes: Section 21-5200

21-5205 Intoxication.

21-5207 Ignorance or mistake.

21-5210 Liability for crimes of another.

21-5220 Use of force; construction and application.

21-5222 Use of force in defense of a person.

21-5223 Use of force in defense of dwelling.

21-5225 Use of force in defense of property – not a dwelling.

21-5226 Use of force by an aggressor.

21-5230 No Duty to Retreat; exceptions.

21-5231 Use of force; immunity from prosecution or liability

Kentucky

Reciprocity: Kentucky honors all other state permits

Legal Permit Age: 21 years old

Officer Contact – Required To Inform: NO

Open Carry: Legal

Carrying Loaded Handgun In Vehicle: Legal

Carry Prohibited In These Locations:

- Schools
- Criminal Justice facility
- Courts
- Liquor establishment
- Child care facility
- Government meetings

Deadly Force Laws: Kentucky Revised Statutes: Section 503

503.010 Definitions for chapter.

503.030 Choice of evils.

503.050 Use of physical force in self-protection

503.055 Use of defensive force regarding dwelling, residence, or occupied vehicle -- Exceptions.

503.060 Improper use of physical force in self-protection.

503.070 Protection of another.

503.080 Protection of property.

503.100 Prevention of a suicide or crime.

Louisiana

■ **Honored**
■ **Special Permit ONLY**

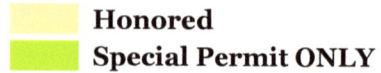

Reciprocity: Lousiana honors the following state permits

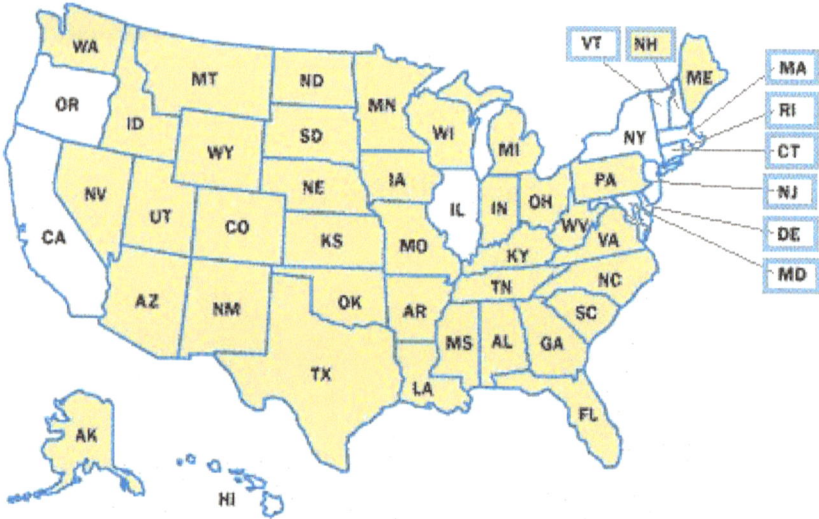

Legal Permit Age: 21 years old

Officer Contact – Required To Inform: YES

Open Carry: Legal

Carrying Loaded Handgun In Vehicle: Legal

Carry Prohibited In These Locations:

- Schools
- Criminal Justice facility
- Courts
- Government meetings
- Polling place
- Church or place of worship

Deadly Force Laws: Louisiana Revised Statutes: Section 14

Maine

Reciprocity: Maine will only honor RESIDENT permits from

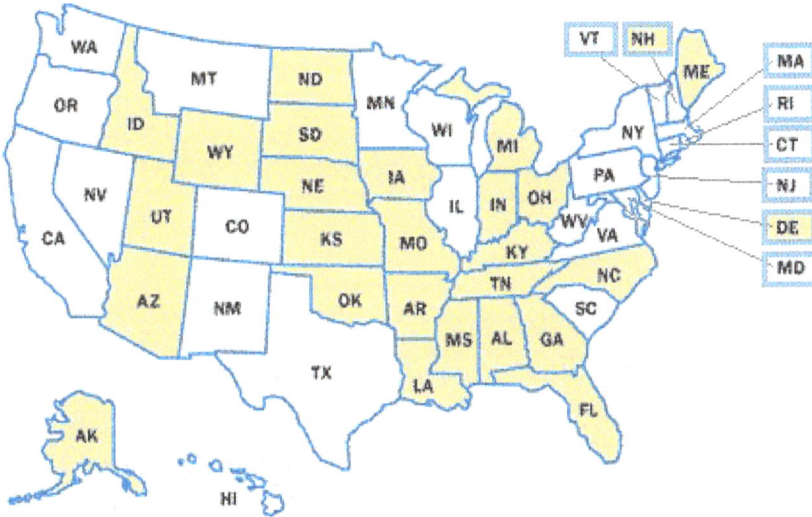

Legal Permit Age: 18 years old

Officer Contact – Required To Inform: YES

Open Carry: Legal

Carrying Loaded Handgun In Vehicle: Legal

Carry Prohibited In These Locations:

- Schools
- Court
- Liquor establishment
- Casino

Deadly Force Laws: Session Laws of Maine: 101-110

Maryland

Reciprocity: Maryland does not honor any other state permits

Legal Permit Age: 18 years old

Officer Contact – Required To Inform: NO

Open Carry: Legal w/ Permit

Carrying Loaded Handgun In Vehicle: Illegal

Carry Prohibited In These Locations:

- Schools
- Legislative buildings

Deadly Force Laws: Code of Maryland

Maryland follows the common law rule that, outside of one's home, a person, before using deadly force in self-defense, has the duty "'to retreat or avoid danger if such means were within his power and consistent with his safety.'"

The duty to retreat also does not apply if one is attacked in one's own home. "[A] man faced with the danger of an attack upon his dwelling need not retreat from his home to escape the danger, but instead may stand his ground and, if necessary to repel the attack, may kill the attacker."

Massachusetts

Reciprocity: Massachusetts does not honor any other state permits

Legal Permit Age: 21 years old

Officer Contact – Required To Inform: NO

Open Carry: Illegal

Carrying Loaded Handgun In Vehicle: Legal

Carry Prohibited In These Locations:

- Schools
- Courts

Deadly Force Laws: Code of Massachusetts

Chapter 233: Section 23F. Admissibility of past physical, sexual or psychological abuse of defendant

Chapter 278: Section 8A. Killing or injuring a person unlawfully in a dwelling; defense

Michigan

Reciprocity: Michigan honors all other RESIDENT state permits

Legal Permit Age: 21 years old

Officer Contact – Required To Inform: YES

Open Carry: Legal w/ Permit

Carrying Loaded Handgun In Vehicle: Illegal

Carry Prohibited In These Locations:

- Schools
- Child care facility
- Stadium or arena
- Casino
- Hospital
- Liquor establishment
- Church or place of worship
- Venue seating more than 2,500 people

Deadly Force Laws: Michigan Compiled Laws

750.200

600.2922

768.21c

780.951

780.971-974

Minnesota

Reciprocity: Minnesota honors the following state permits

*Enhanced / Class 1 Permits ONLY

Legal Permit Age: 21 years old

Officer Contact – Required To Inform: NO

Open Carry: Legal w/ Permit

Carrying Loaded Handgun In Vehicle: Illegal

Carry Prohibited In These Locations:

- Schools / School buses
- Child care facility
- Correctional facility / Courts
- Legislative building
- Any place where signs prohibit

Deadly Force Laws: Minnesota Statutes: Section 609.06

Mississippi

Reciprocity: Mississippi honors all other state permits

Legal Permit Age: 21 years old

Officer Contact – Required To Inform: NO

Open Carry: Legal

Carrying Loaded Handgun In Vehicle: Legal

Carry Prohibited In These Locations:

- Schools
- Criminal Justice facility
- Courts
- Polling place
- Liquor establishments
- Church or place of worship
- Place of "nuisance" (brothels, etc.)
- Any place where signs prohibit

Deadly Force Laws: Mississippi Code: Section 97-3

Missouri

Reciprocity: Missouri honors all other state permits

Legal Permit Age: 19 years old

Officer Contact – Required To Inform: NO

Open Carry: Legal w/ Permit

Carrying Loaded Handgun In Vehicle: Legal

Carry Prohibited In These Locations:

- Schools
- Criminal Justice facility
- Polling place
- Courts
- Government meetings
- Liquor establishments
- Child care facility
- Riverboat gaming facility
- Church or place of worship
- Stadium or arena
- Any place where signs prohibit

Deadly Force Laws: Missouri Revised Statutes: Section 563

563.026. Justification generally.

563.031. Use of force in defense of persons.

563.032. Battered spouse syndrome evidence that defendant acted in self-defense or defense of another-- procedure.

563.036. Use of physical force in defense of premises.

563.041. Use of physical force in defense of property.

563.070 Accidents an excuse for crime, when.

Montana

Reciprocity: Montana honors the following state permits:

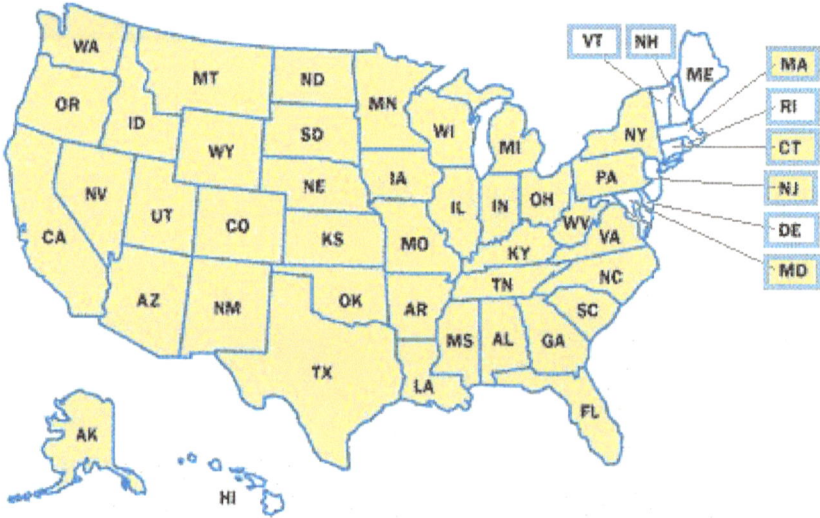

Legal Permit Age: 18 years old

Officer Contact – Required To Inform: NO

Open Carry: Legal

Carrying Loaded Handgun In Vehicle: Legal

Carry Prohibited In These Locations:

- Schools
- State or local government buildings
- Liquor establishment
- Banking or loan institutions

Deadly Force Laws: Montana Code: Section 45-3

Nebraska

Reciprocity: Nebraska honors the following state permits:

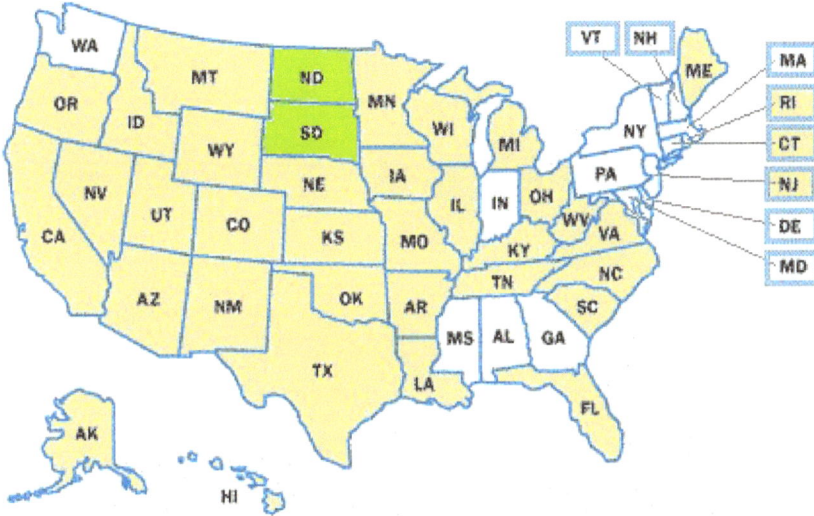

Legal Permit Age: 21 years old

Officer Contact – Required To Inform: YES

Open Carry: Legal

Carrying Loaded Handgun In Vehicle: Illegal unless visible

Carry Prohibited In These Locations:

- Schools
- Criminal Justice facilities / Courts
- Polling places
- Financial institution
- Hospital
- Church or place of worship
- Liquor establishment

Deadly Force Laws: Nebraska Code: Section 28-1400

Nevada

Honored

Special Permit ONLY

Reciprocity: Nevada honors the following state permits:

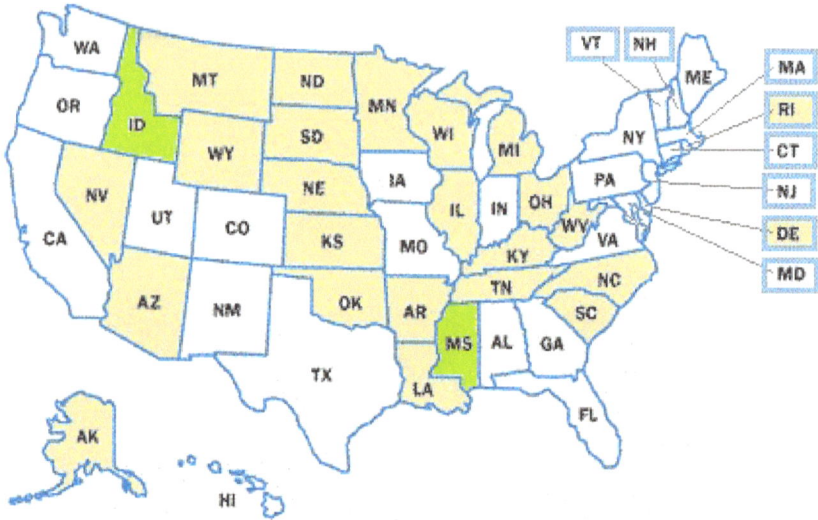

Legal Permit Age: 21 years old

Officer Contact – Required To Inform: NO

Open Carry: Legal

Carrying Loaded Handgun In Vehicle: Legal

Carry Prohibited In These Locations:

- Schools
- Child care facility
- Any place where signs prohibit

Deadly Force Laws: Nevada Revised Statutes: Section 200

New Hampshire

Reciprocity: New Hampshire honors RESIDENT permits of the following states:

Legal Permit Age: No minimum age defined

Officer Contact – Required To Inform: NO

Open Carry: Legal

Carrying Loaded Handgun In Vehicle: Illegal

Carry Prohibited In These Locations:

- Courts

Deadly Force Laws: New Hampshire Statutes: Section 627

New Jersey

Reciprocity: New Jersey does not honor any other state permits

Legal Permit Age: 21 years old

Officer Contact – Required To Inform: NO

Open Carry: Illegal

Carrying Loaded Handgun In Vehicle: Illegal

Carry Prohibited In These Locations:

- Schools
- Casino

Deadly Force Laws: New Jersey Statutes Annotate

2C:3-1. Justification an Affirmative Defense; Civil Remedies Unaffected

2C:3-2. Necessity and other justifications in general

2C:3-3. Execution of public duty

2C:3-4 Use of force in self-protection.

2C:3-5. Use of force for the protection of other persons

2C:3-6. Use of force in defense of premises or personal property

2C:3-9. Mistake of law as to unlawfulness of force or legality of arrest; reckless or negligent use of excessive but otherwise justifiable force; reckless or negligent injury or risk of injury to innocent persons

2C:3-10. Justification in property crimes

New Mexico

Honored

Special Permit ONLY

Reciprocity: New Mexico honors the following state permits:

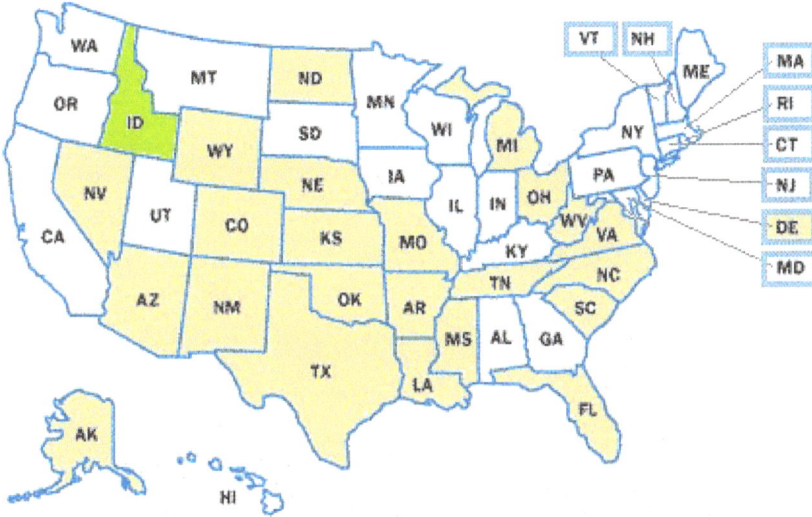

Legal Permit Age: 21 years old

Officer Contact – Required To Inform: NO

Open Carry: Legal

Carrying Loaded Handgun In Vehicle: Legal

Carry Prohibited In These Locations:

- Schools
- Courts
- Tribal land
- Public buses
- Any place where signs prohibit

Deadly Force Laws: New Mexico Statutes: Section 30-2

New York

Reciprocity: New York doe not honor any other state permits

Legal Permit Age: 21 years old

Officer Contact – Required To Inform: NO

Open Carry: Illegal

Carrying Loaded Handgun In Vehicle: Illegal

Carry Prohibited In These Locations:

- Schools
- Courts
- Government buildings

Deadly Force Laws: New York Penal Law

35.00 - Justification; a defense.

35.05 - Justification; generally

35.10 - Justification; use of physical force generally.

35.15 - Justification; use of physical force in defense of a person.

35.20 - Justification; use of physical force in defense of premises and in defense of a person in the course of burglary.

35.25 - Justification; use of physical force to prevent or terminate larceny or criminal mischief.

35.27 - Justification; use of physical force in resisting arrest prohibited.

35.30 - Justification; use of physical force in making an arrest or in preventing an escape.

North Carolina

Reciprocity: North Carolina honors all other state permits

Legal Permit Age: 21 years old

Officer Contact – Required To Inform: YES

Open Carry: Legal but local laws prohibit in some areas

Carrying Loaded Handgun In Vehicle: Illegal

Carry Prohibited In These Locations:

- Schools
- State buildings
- Criminal Justice facilities
- Any place where signs prohibit

Deadly Force Laws: North Carolina General Statutes

§ 14-51.2. Home, Workplace, and Motor Vehicle Protection; Presumption of Fear of Death or Serious Bodily Harm.

§ 14-51.3. Use of Force in Defense of Person; Relief from Criminal or Civil Liability.

§ 14-51.4. Justification for Defensive Force Not Available

North Dakota

Honored
Special Permit ONLY

Reciprocity: North Dakota honors the following state permits

Legal Permit Age: 18 years old

Officer Contact – Required To Inform: NO

Open Carry: Legal w/ Permit

Carrying Loaded Handgun In Vehicle: Illegal

Carry Prohibited In These Locations:

- Church or place of worship
- Liquor establishment
- Athletic or sporting event

Deadly Force Laws: North Dakota Century Code:

Section 12.1-05

Ohio

Reciprocity: Ohio honors all other state permits

Legal Permit Age: 21 years old

Officer Contact – Required To Inform: YES

Open Carry: Legal w/ Permit

Carrying Loaded Handgun In Vehicle: Illegal

Carry Prohibited In These Locations:

- Schools
- Criminal Justice facilities
- Courts
- Mental health facilities
- Child care facilities
- Church or place of worship
- Government buildings
- Liquor establishment (if consuming)

Deadly Force Laws: Ohio Revised Code

§ 2305.40. Immunity of owner, lessee or renter of real property as to self-defense or defense of others.

§ 2307.60 Civil action for damages for criminal act.

§ 2307.601 No duty to retreat in residence or vehicle.

§ 2901.05 Burden of proof - reasonable doubt - self-defense.

§ 2901.09 No duty to retreat in residence or vehicle.

Oklahoma

Reciprocity: Oklahoma honors all other state permits

Legal Permit Age: 21 years old

Officer Contact – Required To Inform: YES

Open Carry: Legal w/ Permit

Carrying Loaded Handgun In Vehicle: Illegal

Carry Prohibited In These Locations:

- Schools
- Government buildings
- Criminal Justice facilities
- Stadium or arena
- Casino
- Buses
- Liquor establishment

Deadly Force Laws: Oklahoma Statutes

§21-643 Force Against Another Not Unlawful, When - Self-Defense - Defense Of Property.

§21-731 Excusable Homicide

§21-733 Justifiable Homicide by Any Person

§21-1289.25 Physical or Deadly Force Against Intruder

Oregon

Reciprocity: Oregon does not honor any other state permits

Legal Permit Age: 21 years old

Officer Contact – Required To Inform: NO

Open Carry: Legal but restricted by most local laws

Carrying Loaded Handgun In Vehicle: Illegal

Carry Prohibited In These Locations:

- Schools
- Corrections facilities
- Race track
- Tribal land

Deadly Force Laws: Oregon Revised Statutes

161.200 Choice of evils.

161.205 Use of physical force generally.

161.209 Use of physical force in defense of a person.

161.215 Limitations on use of physical force – defense of a person.

161.219 Limitations on use of deadly force – defense of a person.

161.225 Use of physical force in defense of premises.

161.229 Use of physical force in defense of property.

161.249 Use of physical force by private person assisting an arrest.

161.265 Use of physical force to prevent escape.

Pennsylvania

Honored
RESIDENT ONLY

Reciprocity: Pennsylvania honors the following state permits

Legal Permit Age: 21 years old

Officer Contact – Required To Inform: NO

Open Carry: Legal w/ Permit

Carrying Loaded Handgun In Vehicle: Illegal

Carry Prohibited In These Locations:

- Schools
- Courts
- Correctional facilities
- Mental health facilities

Deadly Force Laws: Pennsylvania Consolidated Statutes:

501-510

Rhode Island

Reciprocity: Rhode Island does not honor any other state permits

Legal Permit Age: 21 years old

Officer Contact – Required To Inform: NO

Open Carry: Legal w/ Permit

Carrying Loaded Handgun In Vehicle: Illegal

Carry Prohibited In These Locations:

- While under the influence of alcohol or narcotics

Deadly Force Laws: Rhode Island General Laws

§ 11-8-8 Injury or Death – Defense.

South Carolina

Reciprocity: South Carolina honors these RESIDENT permits

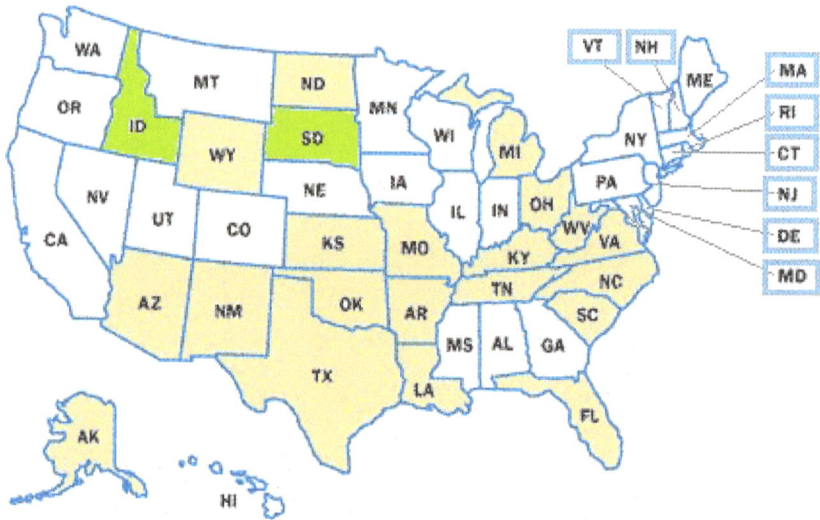

Legal Permit Age: 21 years old

Officer Contact – Required To Inform: YES

Open Carry: Illegal

Carrying Loaded Handgun In Vehicle: Legal

Carry Prohibited In These Locations:

- Schools / Athletic events
- Criminal Justice facilities
- Church or place of worship
- Hospital / Medical facility
- Any place prohibited by signs
- Child care facility
- Polling place
- Government building
- Liquor establishment

Deadly Force Laws: South Carolina Code: Section 16-11-400

South Dakota

Reciprocity: South Dakota honors all other state permits

Legal Permit Age: 18 years old

Officer Contact – Required To Inform: NO

Open Carry: Legal

Carrying Loaded Handgun In Vehicle: Illegal

Carry Prohibited In These Locations:

- Schools
- Liquor establishment
- Courts

Deadly Force Laws: South Dakota Codified Laws

22-16-30 Excusable homicide--Lawful acts.

22-16-31 Excusable homicide--Heat of passion--Provocation--Sudden combat--Limitations.

22-16-32 Justifiable Homicide-Law enforcement officers or at command of officer—Overcoming resistance

22-16-33 Justifiable homicide--Apprehending felon--Suppressing riot--Preserving peace.

22-16-34 Justifiable homicide--Resisting attempted murder--Resisting felony on person or in dwelling house.

22-16-35. Justifiable homicide--Defense of person--Defense of other persons in household.

22-18-4 Justifiable use of force to protect property--Use of deadly force--Duty to retreat

Tennessee

Reciprocity: Tennessee honors all other state permits

Legal Permit Age: 21 years old

Officer Contact – Required To Inform: NO

Open Carry: Legal w/ Permit

Carrying Loaded Handgun In Vehicle: Legal

Carry Prohibited In These Locations:

- Schools
- Courts
- Correctional facilities
- Any place prohibited by signs

Deadly Force Laws: Tennessee Code

39-11-604. Reckless injury of innocent third person.

39-11-609 Necessity.

39-11-610. Public duty.

39-11-611. Self-defense.

39-11-612. Defense of third person.

39-11-613. Protection of life or health.

39-11-614. Protection of property.

39-11-615. Protection of third person's property.

39-11-616. Use of device to protect property.

39-11-621. Use of deadly force by private citizen.

Texas

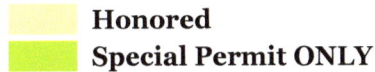

Reciprocity: Texas honors permits from the following states

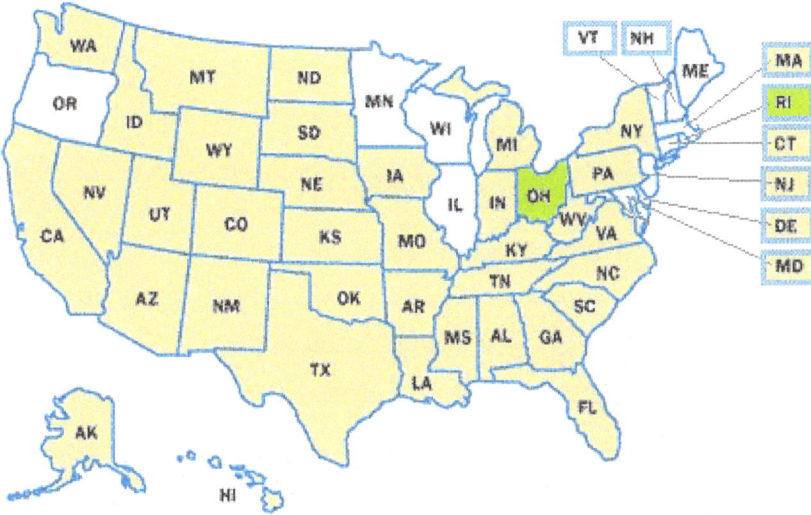

Legal Permit Age: 21 years old

Officer Contact – Required To Inform: YES

Open Carry: Legal w/ Permit

Carrying Loaded Handgun In Vehicle: Legal

Carry Prohibited In These Locations:

- Schools
- Correctional facility
- Liquor establishment
- Hospital or nursing facility
- Amusement park
- Church or place of worship
- Any place signs prohibit

Deadly Force Laws: Texas Statutes: Section 9

Utah

Reciprocity: Utah honors all other state permits

Legal Permit Age: 21 years old

Officer Contact – Required To Inform: NO

Open Carry: Legal w/ Permit

Carrying Loaded Handgun In Vehicle: Legal

Carry Prohibited In These Locations:

- Schools
- Criminal Justice facility
- Mental health facility
- Courts

Deadly Force Laws: Utah Code

76-2-401. Justification as defense - When allowed.

76-2-402. Force in defense of person - Forcible felony defined.

76-2-403. Force in arrest.

76-2-404. Peace officer's use of deadly force.

76-2-405. Force in defense of habitation.

76-2-406. Force in defense of property.

76-2-407. Deadly force in defense of persons on real property.

78B-3-110. Defense to Civil Action for Damages Resulting From Commission of Crime.

Vermont

Reciprocity: Vermont honors all other state permits

Anybody that can legally own a gun in Vermont can carry concealed with no permit required.

Legal Permit Age: 18 years old

Officer Contact – Required To Inform: NO

Open Carry: Legal

Carrying Loaded Handgun In Vehicle: Legal

Carry Prohibited In These Locations:

- Schools
- Courts
- State owned buildings
- Any place prohibited by signs

Deadly Force Laws: Vermont Statutes

§ 2305. Justifiable homicide.

Virginia

Reciprocity: Virginia honors the following state permits

Legal Permit Age: 21 years old

Officer Contact – Required To Inform: NO

Open Carry: Legal

Carrying Loaded Handgun In Vehicle: Legal in a container or compartment of the vehicle (does NOT have to be locked)

Carry Prohibited In These Locations:

- Schools
- Court
- Correctional facility

Deadly Force Laws: Code of Virginia: "Stand-Your Ground"

Duty to retreat only if you are part of the problem.

Washington

Reciprocity: Washington honors the following state permits

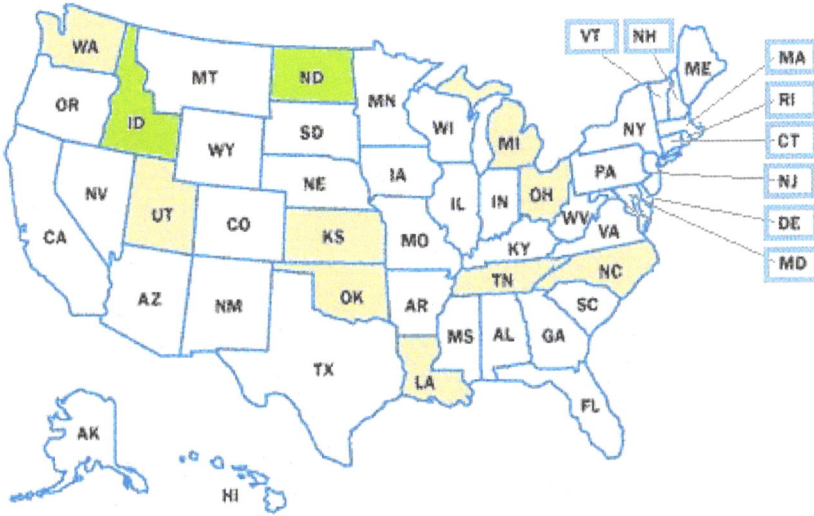

Legal Permit Age: 21 years old

Officer Contact – Required To Inform: NO

Open Carry: Legal

Carrying Loaded Handgun In Vehicle: Illegal

Carry Prohibited In These Locations:

- Schools
- Criminal Justice facility
- Court
- Mental health facility
- Music festival
- Child care facility
- Race track
- Government building
- Liquor establishment

Deadly Force Laws: Revised Code of Washington: Section 9A.16

West Virginia

Reciprocity: West Virginia honors the following state permits

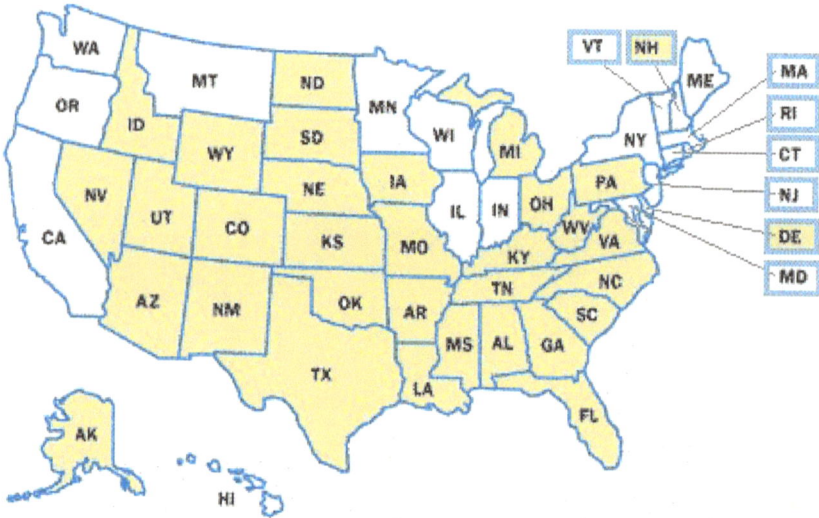

Legal Permit Age: 21 years old

Officer Contact – Required To Inform: NO

Open Carry: Legal

Carrying Loaded Handgun In Vehicle: Legal - Must be in plain view (unless you have a concealed carry permit that is honored)

Carry Prohibited In These Locations:

- Schools
- Courts
- Correctional facility
- Municipal building

Deadly Force Laws: West Virginia Code: Section 55-7-22

Wisconsin

Reciprocity: Wisconsin honors the following state permits

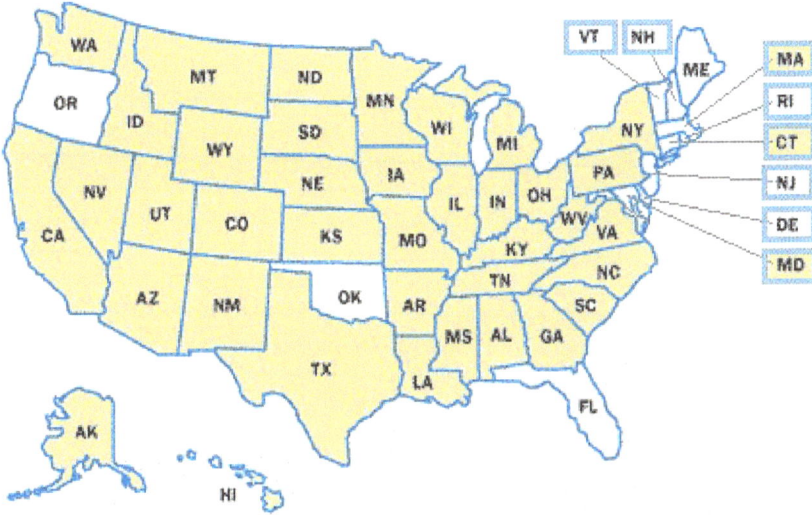

Legal Permit Age: 21 years old

Officer Contact – Required To Inform: NO

Open Carry: Legal

Carrying Loaded Handgun In Vehicle: Legal -Not within 1000 feet of a school

Carry Prohibited In These Locations:

- Schools
- Criminal Justice facility
- Mental health facility
- Courts
- Any place prohibited by signs

Deadly Force Laws: Wisconsin Statutes: Section 939 and 895.62

Wyoming

Reciprocity: Wyoming honors the following state permits

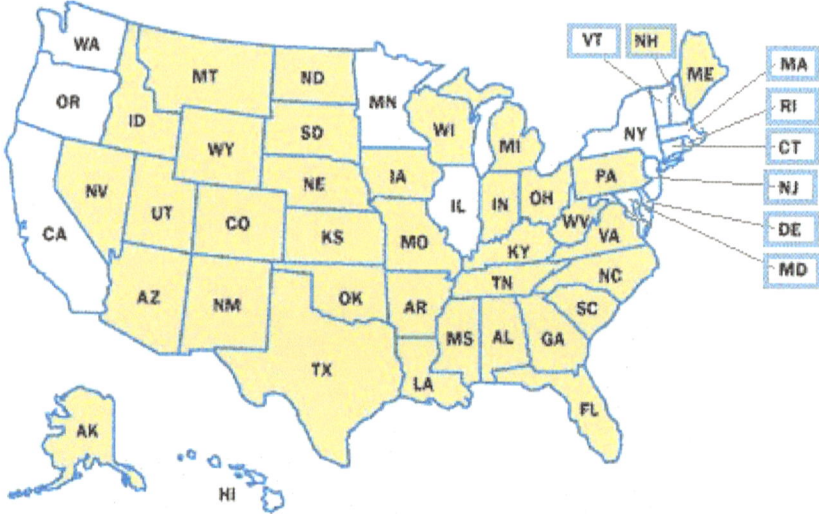

Legal Permit Age: 18 years old

Officer Contact – Required To Inform: NO

Open Carry: Legal

Carrying Loaded Handgun In Vehicle: Illegal

Carry Prohibited In These Locations:

- Schools
- Criminal Justice facility / Court
- Government meetings
- Athletic events
- Liquor establishment
- Church or place of worship
- Any place signs prohibit

Deadly Force Laws: Wyoming Statutes: Section 6-2

This book was published to provide responsible gun owners with a resource for quickly locating laws in whatever jurisdiction they find themselves.

This book does not claim to provide legal advice.

Prior to carrying a firearm in any location, it is solely the responsibility of the owner to know the applicable laws for the area they are in.